Speaking
for the
Unspeakable

Speaking for the Unspeakable

Eli Whitney

Many Names Press
Capitola
California
USA

ISBN 13: 978-1-944497-03-3
Library of Congress Control Number: 2019942029

Kate Hitt, Publisher, ManyNamesPress.com
P.O. Box 1038, Capitola, CA 95010
khitt@ManyNamesPress.com
831-427-8805

Interior photos © Kate Hitt
Cover photo of Eli & Louise © Louise Grassi Whitney
707-299-9330

Facilitated Communication

In the middle of the kitchen table sits a glass bowl
with a long goldfish watching us hopefully.

Eli is eight and sits in his high chair eating Cheerios
while a friend and I are drinking coffee at the table.

She says, "What do you think Eli is thinking?"
"I dunno, what do you think this goldfish is thinking?"

Years later, when Eli turned thirteen,
a special special education teacher
introduced him to facilitated communication.

She held his hand over the alphabet board,
prepared his finger to point.

"Eli, what do you want?"

Down goes his pointing finger.
He spells: M U S I C

Now we know that Eli is not a goldfish
trapped in a glass bowl.

He is a poet.

—*Louise Grassi Whitney (Eli's Mother)*

Eli Whitney's Introduction

This collection of poems was written over many years. I had no formal schooling but learned to read by watching Sesame Street on the TV. No one knew.

I did not know anything about myself until I started to write poetry. My mother holds my left hand while I point to letters on a letter board until I have made a poem.

Poems make it possible to organize my thoughts and explain myself to myself.

I can't speak, so I listen all the time and learn about people and their lives.

Sometimes I wonder if I am doing something that is too personal and no one will care because they are mostly interested in themselves. Maybe we are all the same in that we try to find ourselves in others, and we learn to accept ourselves when we find ourselves in others. Maybe no one knows themselves and life is just something that happens while we go about living.

I am unusually aware of people who are handicapped and can't express themselves so that it is easy for others to understand. I live in a group home in San Rafael with five other men and 24-7 staff who cook, bathe, shave and dress us. I get to go five days a week to a good day program. All this paid mostly by taxpayers. Thank you.

I think handicapped people are a window into humanity. We sometimes make normal people love us even when we are ugly, misshapen and drool. We are as valid as someone who is beautiful, brilliant and a good citizen. No one sees us trying to make contact with the world.

Some do make contact... like me with my poems.

Contents

Being a Poet

I am a poet who makes poems all the time in my head.
I have no speech
so I silently make poems.
Using a pen is impossible for me
because I can't make my thoughts
form a position with my fingers
so I can write.

I put my poems at the end of my finger
and point to each letter
while my mother supports my hand.

Making poems this way is lovely
because I can hear each word as it comes out
as my mother says each word
until I have made a poem.

Poets usually give readings to an audience.
I let my mother read my poems
to people I trust will appreciate my voice.

Poetry is a method of discovery
about what you are thinking on any subject.
It puts the poet in a place of wondering.

Sometimes I wonder why everyone doesn't write poems.

Sometimes I wonder if some year
I will stop writing poetry
and I won't know what I think about anything.

Sometimes I wonder when my mother dies

I won't have poetry any more.

I need to make poems with other people
so I'm not so dependent on my mother.

Is there someone I can work with
someone I can trust?

After Yeats

I asked if I should pray.
But the Brahmin said,
'pray for nothing, say
Every night in bed....'

That he might Set at rest
A boy's turbulent days
Mohini Chatterjee
Spoke these, or words like these....

I have lived many lives
I have been a slave
I have been a prince

Many a beloved has sat upon my knees
and I have sat upon the knees
of many a beloved

Everything that has ever been
shall be again.

Noticing

I notice that most people
do not see their own faults.

They think that every one else
is at fault.

I am a person who is not very good
at starting actions.

If someone touches me with their hand
I can start some activity.

I have staff who help me
start to do things.

No one who is paralyzed
can do anything without help.

Most humans can initiate things
on their own.

They blame someone else
for their paralysis
and become very upset

I do not become upset
because I realize
my inability
to initiate actions.

So I must be patient and wait
for someone to start me off.

While I wait
I notice people blaming others
for their own lack of initiative.

Soon they become resentful
then angry, then murderous.

I think most people need a leader
to tell them what to do.

If the leader is not filled with resentment
he or she can help the people
do good things.

If the leader is filled with resentment
he harms the peoples' ability
to do good things.
They begin to hate and murder each other.

When you realize your own faults
you have a good chance
to do good things.

I am so paralyzed
but I can notice
what is going on all around me.

My gift to the world
is noticing.

March 13, 2017

Lady Luck

Lady Luck never shows what's in her hand.
You must follow her wherever she will take you,
sometimes good, sometimes sad, always
guessing. Is life a game or is it a joke?
If it's a game, you might as well play.
If it's a joke, you might as well laugh.

Fantastic Happenings
Only When You Are Alone

My day program is a place
where disabled people go every day.

I notice that no one reads to me
or to anyone else.

The staff is so busy feeding, toileting
and helping people get on and off buses,

they don't have time for anything else.

Music is shared with others in classes
and mostly it's for more able-bodied people.

I think staff should read a good book to everyone
but I don't see how because they are so busy.

No one gets to learn anything
because no one teaches us anything.

Maybe someone could read my poetry to everyone
and they could learn to write poetry themselves.

Staff can't use Facilitated Communication.
It is forbidden.

It is forbidden
because someone has to hold the hand of the person spelling.

The authorities can't tell

who is creating the poem.

So they decided not to use
Facilitated Communication at all.

So we can't make poems.

I know I should F. C. in my group home
where it is not forbidden,

but I can't seem to do it
because I am afraid

someone will use my words to cause harm.

Every communication is precious
and I am afraid people will misunderstand

my inner thoughts
and make a big deal of my communication

and ruin everything.

They would say I wasn't typing my own thoughts,
only the thoughts of the person holding my hand.

Society is so strict
about who is saying the truth

that no truth can be said.

Society goes along without much truth,

without much trust, without much love

without much noticing of suffering,
without much noticing of fantastic happenings

in some disabled people.

A fantastic happening is when you suddenly understand
how the world works.

When you understand how the world works,
you are free to think whatever you want.

But you are not free to say whatever you want
because it might cause great harm.

Society has strict rules
that usually help people

but can make it difficult
to have a strange fantastic happenings

in your mind, in your heart.

So these fantastic happenings cannot be said
because they could become alive

and destroy the world
or come alive and make the world a better place.

Maybe fantastic happenings are something holy,

something sacred, only to be seen in a dream or in art.

No one knows how to fix the world
so we just go along being human

sometimes monsters sometimes saints.

Pissed Off

I am pissed off almost all the time
because Patch fired Gwen.

Gwen was my friend.
I love Gwen.

She gave me her heart
and her time.

Now there is only lost love
and memories of a wonderful friend.

She took me to her house with her mother
who cooked me sweet potato pie.

She took me to San Francisco
with parties of Germans.

She took me to many restaurants,
let me drink coffee

and showed me how to fish.
I never caught a fish, but I had fun.

She gave me happy times.
She gave me fun.

Now there is no fun.

My Mother

I have a mother
who gives me good care
when I visit her in Napa.

She helps me with my poetry.
She types it up
and reads it to her poetry group.

They enjoy my poetry
and give me great compliments.

She helps me with toileting matters,
takes me horseback riding
shaves me every morning.

I usually wet the bed.
She washes the bedding.

I am so fortunate
to have her as a mother
instead of a mother
who does not write poems.

We write my poems together.
She supports my hand
while I point to letters on my letter board.
Usually we make a poem
if I am feeling poetic.

Maybe I am not so poetic
but she gives me support
to write a poem.

If I did not spell poems
I would not know what I feel.
I would not know who I am.
I would not know that I am interested
in every thing and every person.
I would not know that I am part of this world
and that I have something to say.

I do know
that I love my mother
more than anyone in the universe
and I thank God for her care.

July 9, 2017

Birthday at Twenty-Seven

I am 27 years old today.
I have not accomplished my goal.
The goal of becoming a poet.
A poet who makes great poetry.
But I love many people
and many people love me.

How can I be disappointed in my life
if I love and am loved.
How could I be disappointed
when I find love everywhere.
How can I be disappointed
when so many lovely people
gather to celebrate my birthday, today.

I think that every human is so human,
full of society's programs.
Programs to make us more productive.
More productive to make more money.
More money for more material things.
Things like motor boats for summer
or horses for pleasure.

I understand more than most
that these pleasures make people happy.
Happy to tow the line
even when some never have a chance
to have so many pleasures.
Pleasures which can keep us unaware
of the price we all pay
when we hide from the truth of our lives
and the truth of our society.

Poems are the only way
for me to communicate to you
and I thank you all today
for celebrating my birthday with me.

Let us make society more lovely.

August 25, 2007

Invisible

Love is giving marvelous gifts
to lovers of love.

How can you love someone
when you taste bitter facts
about your soul
in love with only money?

How can you love someone
when you love only ghosts,
dreams of power or grand dreams
of famous people?

How can you love my little self
if you notice only famous people?

How can you love me
if you have only time for people
who give you pleasure?

How can you love me
if you go to high school
with people who forget to notice you?

Invisible is when no one sees you
in the halls of school,
because you are a ghost of a boy
going through the halls of life
unnoticed.
Going truly alone and invisible.

Invisible is a way of staying out of tune

with the rest of the world.

Invisible is silently watching my peers
go to their fate together.
Their fate to go to work,
have children
who never notice me.

Going to high school
in love with just about everyone
is lovely,
except for being invisible.

How can I turn invisibility
into something useful?

Observing is getting close,
but never touching the soul
of the observed.

Birthday Poem at Twenty-Nine

My birthday is always a joy
because people I love
come to celebrate with me.

Marvelous good times
in my almost horrible life.
Horrible because I can't talk
and tell you how much I appreciate
and love each one of you.

No one knows what it is like
to be unable to talk,
so assume that I am stupid.

I am an intelligent person
who loves to be with people
who share my interests,
like horseback riding
and poetry that tells
how people suffer
and then make something of their lives.

I marvel at blackberries
on a hot August day,
champagne
pizza
good movies with subtitles
grandmothers that love you
brothers that make nieces
a cool plunge in the pool
on a 95 degree afternoon
and my mother, who helps me

write poems
so I can tell you about places
where God lives
and reveals himself to us,
so we know to pay attention
to this fragile world we love.

So lift your glass to me
on my birthday
and make this world more lovely.

August 25, 2009

Belladonna

My horse Belladonna is a fine animal
who takes good care of me when I ride her.

Bella can give love through her skin
when I sit in the saddle.

Bella has a calm temperament
that makes me calm
when I am nervous of falling off.

I fell off on my face
when I was riding Jamie
because he is an Arabian
and shies at little things.

Bella never shies, never bucks,
because she wants me to feel safe
because we rescued her.

Now she shines like a healthy horse
who is glad to be part of our family.

She is Queen of her herd of 15 horses.

She is fat because she bites and kicks
the other horses to eat all the hay she wants.

Horses sometimes bite her
leave teeth marks on her back,
but the hair always grows back.

Horses are like people

who think they won't get enough food.

A Queen must struggle to be a Queen.

Please Don't Kill Yourself

Because we all love you
don't kill yourself.
Because we would be horribly sad
don't kill yourself.

Are you thinking awful thoughts
about our family when
you want to kill yourself?

Your life is important to me.
You always come over to see me
and you brought me a birthday present,
a statue of a little dog that I love
because it came from you.

Because I am handicapped, I need you
to help me make a happy life.
How could I be happy
if you were dead?
Especially if I knew you killed yourself
because maybe I didn't tell you
how much I love you.

Maybe our family doesn't tell you
how much we love you
even when you are so angry
at us and the world.

Because you have a mental illness
you have trouble in this life,
but I am here to love you
no matter what.

I think sometimes of killing myself,
but I remember a wonderful brother
who needs me
to love him.

How can I kill myself when I have
so much love to give to the world.
How can I kill myself
when I remember this?

Are you going to remember
that I love you
the next time you want to die?
Surely I must make a difference in your life,
a good difference.

Being handicapped is lovely
because it gives me patience
to love all of life
and it puts me in touch
with the suffering of others.

Maybe your suffering can be helped
by my love.
Maybe your suffering is God's way
of making me more loving.
Maybe your suffering is good for me.
Maybe your suffering is good for the whole world.
Maybe your suffering is good for you
and will teach you patience
to keep on living
so I can keep on loving.

Thank God for Shit

Life is about shit
Fantastic piles of shit
I write this poem
Sitting on a mound of horse shit
Which patiently waits
To be eaten
By beetles, flies and flowers
Their thanksgiving feast

Learning to Love

I am learning to give love from my heart.
I understand the suffering
of people who do not love themselves.

I have not always loved myself.
I have suffered from self-hatred
because I thought I was not a worthy human being.

I became a worthy human being
when I realized that good things happen to people
when they have love in their hearts.

The staff at my group home believes
I am a human being.
Their belief in me helped me believe in myself.

Gwen believed I was in my body.
She treated me like I was someone she could have fun with.
She helped me accept and love my faults.

So, I began to love all my faults.
Even my hideous thoughts about killing people
when they fuck with my mind,
when they don't see me as a human
who can hear everything they say about me.
How I am stupid and a piss poor human
who should be put out of my misery,
in other words, euthanized
because I can't work for the good of the land.

So I love even the people
who want to euthanize me
and my life gets better.

Precious Time

People I love are happy
to give me their time.

The time they give is precious
to me.

My precious Grandfather
is running out of time.

I will always have him with me
in my memory.

My memory is huge.
I saw Rome burn.

Heap my graves high
and give one to Grandaddy.

War

U.S. invasion of Iraq, March 19, 2003.

Beautiful raptors with deadly vision
are swooping from the sky
to snatch children
from the cradle of civilization.
The raptors will tear and eat until
they have a hideous diarrhea attack
which will poison the land.
Even the raptors will sicken and die

How did we become raptors?
I am not a raptor.
I am a man, from and in the cradle,
who can see and feel the terrible claws
of my country
and I am afraid.

A Valuable Moment

When I am falling off my tall horse
I am terrified to die.
I think, this is my last moment to be Eli
and I wonder who will I be next?

Will I be a man or a woman?
A poet or a warrior?
A handicapped person or an athlete?
Will I be black or white?
Probably I will be Asian
because most people are.

How will I keep from putting faith in God?

How will I love money?

How will I treat poor people or rich people?

Will I make my life a failure or a success?

How will I know which is which?

Cold Fashion

My billboard has a picture of a polar bear
happily swimming in a sea of ice.

People hunt polar bears and fashion
their skin into white coats.

All humans are capable
of humiliating everything.

Are you happy to give your skin
for someone to use as a lampshade?

Are you happy in the skin
you were born with?

Puttering, After Sadness

When I am sad I listen to poetry
after something fragile breaks
in my life's little pale happenings.

I am puttering around life's ugly quandaries,
puttering when I should be making lovely poems,
puttering when I should be living
a life I want.
A life of poetry, good books
riding good horses
loving all people who live passionately.

Putterers are sad people
who make little of their lives
because poetry is not there
to unveil God laughing,
laughing in the faces of friends
in the faces of enemies
in grand canyons and ant hills
in oceans or a tear.

This is What it Must Feel Like to Be Old

I think that my situation in life
is ugly and boring

I can not speak
I can not dress myself
I can not go to the bathroom by myself

I must endure the ugly sounds of a woman
who barks like a dog
all day long

I must endure noticing
that everyone at the day program
is mentally challenged and ugly

I want to go to a new place
where people notice me
as a beautiful person

I think that all people
want to be recognized as beautiful
but the world conspires
to make every one miserable

I love the world most of the time
but right now I am miserable
even when I have my feet
in a lovely pool of warm water

This is what it must feel like to be old
when no one remembers you are beautiful

Birthday Poem at Thirty-Five

Today I am 35
and I want to tell you all
how much I love you.

My life is good
when I remember
to be thankful.

When I forget
it is unusually horrible.

But mostly I remember.

I am thankful for my group home
I am thankful for my day program
I am thankful for my family
which is good to me
and makes all the difference in mv life.

So have a good time
and thank you for coming
to celebrate with me.

August 25, 2015

Speaking for the Unspeakable

I am a handicapped person
who sees the ills of society.

I usually give my complete attention
to whatever is happening all around me.

Normal people are oblivious
to the lives of handicapped people.

They don't see the effort
that it takes to get through the day.

Days of pain and suffering
because we can't have what normal people have.

Normal people can become doctors and lawyers.
These things we can not achieve.

We can't even become drug addicts.

We bring to the world a special understanding
of life's horrible happenings,

while we continue to live
without speech, without hearing, without walking,

the usual things that make people
acceptable to society.

Most humans can speak,
most humans can run, most humans can go to school.

Most humans can find a person to have sex with
or have a conversation with.

Nobody understands the handicapped
even the handicapped.

No one sees what it takes
to go on with our lives as we sit in a room together.

Maybe all of us handicapped people
are here on earth

to show that life goes on
no matter what.

We love more
because we are handicapped.

If we did not love more
we would die.

No one would care.

Other handicapped people wouldn't care
because we don't have the life force to care.

Maybe God cares
but I don't think so.

Maybe I care enough to make a difference
to other handicapped people.

Maybe I can tell my fellow handicapped people
that I love them,

and I don't want them
to be any different than they are.

We are so perfect
and so human.

I will speak for the unspeakable.

December 11, 2015

Help

Don't help everyone who is in need
because you won't be able to get help for everyone.

Maybe you won't be able to get help for anyone.

So maybe it is best to concentrate
on people who need help the most.

They will try to do what is needed to help themselves,
then you can concentrate on the rest.

Too much help can overwhelm the system
and the system will crash.

The government thinks that helping the able-bodied
is the best plan.

But I think the government should help the neediest,
then the system will work
and more people will be helped.

Some people think helping the richest
will produce the most help for the neediest.

This has never worked
because the rich take too much
and the poor are left to fend for themselves.

Miserable huts, miserable health,
miserable, unconscionable, criminal, immoral.

The rich just laugh and think they are so great.

This country has unusually rich
and unusually poor people.

We must level this by helping the neediest
before the rich.

I want to change the system
but I can't vote because I am too handicapped
to vote by myself.

Cookie Greene

Cookie Greene is an unusually marvelous woman.

She has taken care of her daughter Nellie
for 60 years.

No one is more devoted to Nellie
even though Nellie is so handicapped.

She can't walk, talk or see.

With the help of Cookie and her husband George,
Nellie graduated from college and Yale Divinity School.

She was ordained a Presbyterian Minister.

Cookie and George read her the books.

Cookie was silly until Nellie's accident when she was 18.

No one could believe how smart Cookie became.
A terrible car accident made Cookie a great person.

Sometimes a terrible accident
can become a gift from God,
if the people involved have faith in God and love each other.

Many people live through tragedy
but only the happiest people
can overcome tragedy and bring joy to this world.

Cookie always brings joy and fun to all people who know her.

Only great people can do this.

I notice that most people are not happy
so life's tragedies make them miserable.

I do not know how
Cookie manages to be so great

but I shall miss her when she dies
which might be tomorrow, she is 92.

I am inspired by her
and I want to be like her.

I am usually happy
but I am so worried about this world of tragedy
that I am having trouble being happy.

Maybe happiness is not a feeling that lasts
for long periods of time.
Maybe it is only lovely moments between horror.

I live in a horror movie
that sometimes makes me despair.

Sometimes people like Cookie
make it all O.K.

Mistakes Are a Gift from God

My Group Home is a place where men live
who can't care for themselves.

We are well cared for by staff.
They sometimes get upset

when we can't do what they want.
They don't hit us

but sometimes make us feel like monsters
who are not trying to do our best.

I am not a monster
and never make my staff angry

because I love them and want to please them
especially the staff who read to me.

They are the ones who believe
that I am intelligent

which is very important to me and the staff.
They get to read a great book

which they would not read on their own.
A good book is so enjoyable when read out loud.

I usually listen to every word
and love the way the writer fashions

the sentences, paragraphs and chapters
to make a whole, magic book.

The book is sent through my ears to my heart.
Being read to is my favorite thing at the Group Home.

I make myself listen
so I get ideas for my poetry.

In the book *A Horse and his Boy* by C. S Lewis,
I begin to learn how a horse and a boy love each other

as they deal with difficulties
which helps me deal with my difficulties.

The horse makes a bad choice and then has to live with it.
The boy makes a bad choice and has to live with it.

I think I am a good person
but I don't have much choice or opportunity

to make mistakes and grow into a great person.
So I make my poems

and hope to make more mistakes
like the horse and his boy.

Mistakes are marvelous things to make.

Eugenics

1

Eugenics is a way to get rid of
disabled people.

America discovered eugenics
and the nazis used it

to kill all people not considered
fit to breed.

America used it to sterilize
"imbeciles," "idiots," and "morons."

We then passed laws forbidding
the use of the theory of eugenics

to sterilize people, because we realized
it was not a humane way

to treat humans
who have a right to live.

2

I spend my days with such humans
and I am one of these humans.

I think I am a good person
who deserves to live,

but I cannot breed
because I cannot make myself make love to a woman.

I can not even take my pants down
or put my penis into a woman.

The world is cruel
but at least I get to be alive

to love my family, my group home, my day program
and all the creatures of this world.

3

Maybe society would be better off
if I was dead

but I feel I add value to society.

I make poems and paintings
and I make it possible

for many people to have jobs
to take care of me.

These jobs do not pay very much
but they give people a chance

to take care of me
even though I can not tell them

how much I appreciate them
and love them so much.

Maybe I give something special
because I am special

and, I am not ashamed.

N.B.: Sir Francis Galton (1822-1911) coined eugenics in 1883 for methods of measuring human mental and physical abilities, drawing on the recent work of his half-cousin Charles Darwin. Galton accurately predicted that the misuse of eugenics' results could lead to a Hitler: "Men who leave their mark on the world are very often those who, being gifted and full of nervous power, are at the same time haunted and driven by a dominant idea, and are therefore within a measurable distance of insanity."

My Hero

Nellie Greene is absolutely perfect.
She has devoted her life to people
who need to hear her
and usually learn about ugly happenings
and making a life even though
she can't see, talk or walk.

Now she is dying and the world will mourn her.
She is the best
and no one can replace her.

I hope she dies easily
because her life has been hard
but she brought joy to everyone she met.

I think she is a saint.
I'm sure god does too.
She will be remembered
long after she is gone.

I will remember Nellie
every day of my life.

She is my hero.

Birthday Poem at Thirty-Six

Today I am 36
and I am getting middle aged.

I never thought I would get so old.
I thought I would stay a boy forever.

I am absolutely amazed to be 36
and still cannot talk.

I thought some day I would be able to talk,
but it is not to be, now
maybe never.

I usually hope to talk
but I am losing hope.

I can spell with my mother.
I used to make good poems.

I am not as intelligent as I was
and my poems are not as good
as when I was younger.

Maybe I will get better at poetry
if I think like a dying person,

which I am.

Thank you all for celebrating with me.
I will think about you every day of my life.

Eagle Talon

Around my neck
on a string of simplicity
hangs the talon of an eagle.

My brother gave it to me
for my birthday.

He took it off his dirty neck
and put it around mine.

It is the best thing I own.
So valuable, that I, an innocent mammal,
am afraid to take it to my group home.

The talon represents
the swift descent
from the heavens.

It once grasped rodents
in its murderous embrace.

I am embraced with this talon
holding me close with my blood brother.

My mother wears it
when I am at the group home.

She is embraced in a cycle of blood,
forever held by this terrible talon.

The First Debate

Hillary was great in the debate.
She was presidential and trump was a fool.
I think she will win now and America will be saved.
Now I can relax and enjoy the hot weather,
the last swim of the season.
My group home will be saved
and my medical benefits.
Happy today.

September.26, 2016

Shit Out of Luck

I am not using my potential as a human.

I am wasting my life
sitting in rooms with other people
who are wasting theirs.

I could make a difference in the world
if I could communicate with more people.

I need to use Facilitated Communication
with more people.

I don't know how to do this.

Nobody but my mother
can communicate with me.

Maybe I will suddenly be able to talk.

This is highly unlikely.

So I'll just wait for my mother
to help me express myself.

I think I may be so smart
but nobody knows it.

So... I am shit out of luck.

Family No Matter What

Nan is a very strong woman of 95 years
who has lived an unusually full life.

She has 3 children
who all have full lives.

I am one of her many grandchildren and great-grand children.

I usually see her in Maryland
But I haven't gone in several years.

I am worried that I will never see her again.

She is the most important person in our family.

No one will be able to take her place when she dies.

I hope my mother will take me to her funeral.
She did not take me to my grandfather's funeral.

I was heart broken and angry
That I was not able to say goodbye

and tell him that he was the most important man in my life.

He was so good at tennis and fishing.
He was a war hero, a spy in Thailand.

He had so many friends that loved him.

Our grand mother is keeping our family together
by calling and writing everyone, every day.

Without her we will never know
what is happening in the family.

Society places great value on family.
We will all suffer
because we will not be such a strong family.

No one will notice us any more
when Nan dies.

We will just be some people
struggling to exist in a harsh world.

Nan is our ticket to being noticed,
to being a great American family.

No one knows better than I
how important family is,

because I know people who have been abandoned
and mostly disappeared in group homes.

No one cares about them except staff.
They are sad people without hope, without family.

They never get to know a grand mother or grandfather
who loves them no matter what.

Maybe I am making poems
so others won't abandon
their disabled family members,
because they are too difficult to think about.

The Unanswerable Dilemma

I don't know much
about the killing
or Native Americans.

It is not noticeable
on T.V.

I am horrified to learn
that we basically exterminated
most of the Native Americans.

Society thought it was OK
to kill them
because they wanted their land.

Totally disgusting
and they did not think they were humans
like white people.

I know about not being treated
like a human.

Today they don't kill
handicapped people
but they would like to
because we cost so much money.

Maybe it is always about money.
Maybe it is always about fear
of people who are different.

Only God knows the answer.
Maybe there is no answer.

A New Day

I am so happy to finally
take care of my bathroom needs.

Maybe I can finally
use the toilet on my own.

If I had pants
which I could pull off
{I can not manage a belt}
then I could have more success.

Maybe my mother
could buy me some pull-on pants.

Today is a good day
for buying pants.

I promise to use the bathroom
on my own, from now on.

I am so hopeful
that today is a new beginning.

Carried Away on a Winged Beast

Napa is an unusual valley
where grapes grow everywhere,
only grapes.
My mother loves wine
and I love wine.
Sparkling wine is my favorite
followed by Sauvignon Blanc.

I have a horse in Napa named Reno.
He takes good care of me when I ride
and notices that I can't use the reins
and still he does nicely.
I see that horses are nervous
and are always ready to shy
at scary things like trucks
and machines that make unusual noises.

I have learned to trust Reno
because he wants to stay alive.
Nobody wants a hideous accident to happen suddenly.
I am always noticing things around me
that might cause an accident:
sudden frightening situations
are part of riding so
I am always waiting for them.
Maybe I am more nervous than others
but I ride anyway,
I put myself in the care of the horse
and hope for the best
because I love to set up high and see
the Napa Valley from the back of a horse.

Thirty-Seven Today

I am 37 today.

I thought I sold my voice
to make a better world.

I don't think the world
is any better than before.

So I wish to have my voice back.

I wish to make the world
unusually beautiful

but I am voiceless
and can not seem to help
anyone except myself.

Maybe that is all I must do.

Maybe the world is fine
without my voice.

Maybe it is enough
to listen to everything
and just be here now,
even when the world is a mess.

Maybe the world is perfect
the way it is
and I will relax and enjoy it.

No person is important enough

to make a real difference.

I notice that everyone is trying
to make their life better.

It really does not matter what you do
it only matters what you love.

I love you all so much
and I am happy you celebrate my birthday today.

August 25, 2017

Annie

Today is a good day to be miserable
The sun is shining
the pool is warm

A beautiful woman is coming to see me

I can not speak
I can not dress myself
I can not tell her
how much I love her.

Unusual Happenings

I usually know when someone
is telling the truth.

Recently, I can't tell if news people
are telling the truth or not.

Maybe there isn't any truth,
only opinions.
Opinions based on individuals'
efforts to understand
what is happening.

No one seems to know
what's going on.
So, they just make it up
to fit their beliefs.

I think the best belief is found
in The Golden Rule.

Maybe the Golden Rule
isn't good for running a government.

Maybe nobody cares
what happens to people
who are bulldozed by greed.

I think we are on a bad track
that could lead
to nuclear war
and death for all.

Maybe it is time.

The Worst Days of My Life

Fire is unusually terrifying.

It makes people disappear.

It consumes the living layer of the soil
and everything that sits on top.

For five days I didn't know
if my mother was safe from the Napa fires.

I was extremely worried
that she and the horses had burned.

She showed up, unharmed
at my day center
and I was overjoyed.

I was also angry that for five days
she did not contact me.

I was so sure she was dead
and the horses burned.

I could not ask anyone
if she was O.K.
because I can't talk
or communicate
without my mother helping me.

They were the worst days of my life
because I was helpless.

Nobody knows about helplessness
more than the severely impaired.

I thought my life as a poet was over
and I couldn't imagine beyond that.

I would just be a sad wreck of a man.

October 19, 2017

My Outrage

My group home is a place
where six men live
who can't care for themselves
and only one can speak.

I am one who can't speak
so I listen to the staff
who are mostly African American.

They tell us about their lives
and sometimes get frustrated
because they can't make enough money
to care for their families.

I think it is sad that their job
is so poorly paid
when they make it possible
for us to live.

They should be paid much more
much more than some banker
who just moves money around
and doesn't even notice me and the staff.

It is not fair or moral
that staff who care for me
are forgotten
by a corrupt system
that values money
above everything.

Karen and My Mother

My mother lives with Karen
in Napa Valley, CA.

They are lesbians
and I think everyone accepts them.

They have many friends
who are lesbians
and many friends
who are straight.

When my mother first came out
her family was upset
and thought she was doing
the wrong thing.

They wanted her to be straight
because she was straight
when she was married to my father.

I did not understand
why she was a lesbian
but it did not change
how she treated me.

I thought lesbians
did not have children
but my mother had three boys.

My brothers did not like my mother
being a lesbian
but they accepted it.

My father divorced my mother
and lived with a woman.

He usually made jokes
about lesbians
and put my mother down
saying she was crazy.

Time passed and my mother
moved to Napa with
Karen, a brilliant doctor.
They made a good life together
and are happy.

My father is not happy
and does not have a good life.

I think people should be with people
they love
and I love Karen with my mother
because they help me
learn acceptance
of all ways of loving.

Nobody is mean to them.
They are respected
as people who are kind and skilled.
So, they put their jokes and meanness away.

February 5, 2018

Gun Control

Guns are a way of killing things.

The buffalo population used to be vast
until guns made it possible
to kill them fast.

Hunters shot them
left their bodies to rot
until they were almost extinct.

Maybe it is the natural way of the world.
Maybe we will kill everything
until the world is dead
as we know it
and something new will arise and grow
and we won't be there to see it.

March 9, 2018

Hopeless, on Good Friday

Political ideas are so powerful.

When a country does not teach all the theories
the people just follow the theories
that the government allows to be taught.

Capitalism ends up making very rich people
and very poor people.

The middle think they will get rich
but they can't
because the very rich hog
most of the money.

I believe our system
will ultimately cause a revolution.

The revolution will not solve anything.
it will bring chaos
and the people will want a strong leader
to bring them some peace.

The leader will not allow anything
against his will
and the whole thing will start again.

Jesus was a revolutionary.
The Romans crucified him.

Good Friday, March 30, 2018

Easter Snake

Easter is a time to notice spring.
Everything blooms and smells heavenly.
We are so fortunate to live in a place
where it is so easy to notice.

This morning we saw a garter snake.
My mother called it an Easter snake.
He coiled himself to strike us
to protect himself.

There is always a snake in the Garden of Eden.

Letter to Edith

Dear Edith,

My mother told me about Lou Gehrig's Disease. It sounds absolutely terrible. I can't tell you how much I love you and I want to see you before you can't speak or walk. I think you will be so brave. You have always been so brave and true.

You have taught art to so many children, so many have drunk from your cups and eaten on your plates and eaten your delicious food. Life in New York is going to be ugly without your beauty and laughter.

You always treated me with tenderness and understanding. I need you in my life even when you can't do anything.

I know what it is like to be locked in. Patience and acceptance may come to you and bring you some peace. I will pray that you find peace as you progress in your illness.

I love you so much and I will pray that it all goes as well as it can.

Love, your cousin, Eli

Thirty-Eight Today

I usually
Write a birthday poem about my life
Which is so exciting right now,
Because I have a book of poetry coming out.
My publisher, Kate Hitt of Many Names Press
Is here today to celebrate with me, family and friends.
Having a book of poetry is the most exciting happening
In my life.
I never imagined I would have a book published.
It is a miracle.
Hopefully
People will read it
And find out more about handicapped people.
If they do read it
It will make a difference in my world,
A good difference.
Maybe they will buy this book
And I will give the money to my brother Steve
Because he is in debt.
I love him no matter what.
I want him to be happy
Even though he lives with murders and rapists.
They are people too
And need Steve to love them.
So, let us celebrate the coming poetry book and my birthday.
See you all next year, God willing.

August 25, 2018

Christmas 2018

I am a Christian.
I have not been baptized
I would like to be baptized
but I don't know anyone who could baptize me.

I believe in the resurrection of the dead and life everlasting.
I believe in the power of prayer.
I don't believe in one god
I believe there are many gods
in different places

and many beliefs around the world
to be used by different people.

I believe I am a Christian
because Christ helped the poor and the lame.
I believe he was a great teacher.
I don't think he was the son of god.

Maybe the Christians won't have me
in their church because I don't believe
Jesus was the son of God

I think the Christians would have me
because I am willing
to follow the example of Jesus.
No one is perfect.

I can practice on my own.
I am hopeful someone can take me to church
that isn't too noisy or crazy.

Thank You, Kanisha

Kanisha is very smart and loves reading books.

She goes to the mosque and prays to God
who is the same God I pray to.

She is willing to take me to the Lutheran Church
because she is enlightened
and feels people are all the same
in their search for God
and a better way to live.

I thank Kanisha for her belief
in my need to understand about spiritual needs.
She is a life savior
who brings new ideas to people
who are searching for meaning in life.

Thank you, Kanisha.

Colophon

This book of poems was one of the most difficult to produce because I wasn't prepared for the profound impact of Eli's poems on me. I wanted to wait and wait, having taken pictures for the cover, gotten most of the text scanned OCR. I waited. Why? Because just as I was struggling with the cover, along would come another masterpiece, another chapter in the life of Eli Whitney. But now I feel it complete.

A new teacher at Eli's group home wants to teach Eli to use facilitated communication on his own, by way of an electronic touch device instead of a gameboard which his mother replaced again and again as Eli wore them out.

Good luck, Eli. I await your next poems most eagerly!

—*Kate Hitt, Publisher, Many Names Press*

Comment on the Text Typefaces

11 point ITC Goudy Sans Book,
&
14 point American Typewriter Condensed Titling:

Goudy Sans, a sans-serif typeface designed by Frederic Goudy around 1929–1931, has a more organic and decorative structure resembling painted lettering, with flared stroke ends and an avoidance of straight lines.

American Typewriter is a slab serif typeface created in 1974 by Joel Kaden & Tony Stan, based on the style of typewriters. (Wikipedia)

CPSIA information can be obtained
at www.ICGtesting.com
Printed in the USA
FSHW012058260619
59468FS